Jewellery Making Journal

Dear Zaha,
Merry Christmas,
May you make loads of jewellery!
with love
Maria xxx
25.12.19.

All rights reserved. This book or any portion thereof may not be reproduced or used in any manner whatsoever without the express written permission of the author.

ISBN: 9781730950797

© Just Plan Books. All rights reserved.

Item Name:

NOTES

COMPONENTS	QTY	COST
	TOTAL COST	
	SELLING PRICE	

Item Name:

DESIGN PORTFOLIO

NOTES

COMPONENTS | QTY | COST

TOTAL COST
SELLING PRICE

Item Name:

NOTES

COMPONENTS	QTY	COST
	TOTAL COST	
	SELLING PRICE	

Item Name:

NOTES

DESIGN PORTFOLIO

COMPONENTS	QTY	COST

TOTAL COST
SELLING PRICE

Item Name:

NOTES

COMPONENTS	QTY	COST
	TOTAL COST	
	SELLING PRICE	

Item Name:

NOTES

COMPONENTS | QTY | COST

TOTAL COST
SELLING PRICE

DESIGN PORTFOLIO

Item Name:

NOTES

COMPONENTS	QTY	COST

TOTAL COST
SELLING PRICE

Item Name:

NOTES

COMPONENTS | QTY | COST

TOTAL COST
SELLING PRICE

DESIGN PORTFOLIO

Item Name:

NOTES

COMPONENTS	QTY	COST

TOTAL COST

SELLING PRICE

Item Name:

DESIGN PORTFOLIO

NOTES

COMPONENTS | QTY | COST

TOTAL COST
SELLING PRICE

Item Name:

NOTES

COMPONENTS	QTY	COST
	TOTAL COST	
	SELLING PRICE	

Item Name:

NOTES

DESIGN PORTFOLIO

COMPONENTS	QTY	COST

TOTAL COST
SELLING PRICE

Item Name:

NOTES

COMPONENTS | QTY | COST

TOTAL COST
SELLING PRICE

Item Name:

NOTES

COMPONENTS	QTY	COST
TOTAL COST		
SELLING PRICE		

DESIGN PORTFOLIO

Item Name:

NOTES

COMPONENTS	QTY	COST
	TOTAL COST	
	SELLING PRICE	

Item Name:

NOTES

COMPONENTS	QTY	COST
	TOTAL COST	
	SELLING PRICE	

DESIGN PORTFOLIO

Item Name:

NOTES

COMPONENTS	QTY	COST
	TOTAL COST	
	SELLING PRICE	

Item Name:

NOTES

COMPONENTS | QTY | COST

TOTAL COST
SELLING PRICE

DESIGN PORTFOLIO

Item Name:

NOTES

COMPONENTS	QTY	COST

TOTAL COST

SELLING PRICE

Item Name:

NOTES

COMPONENTS | QTY | COST

TOTAL COST
SELLING PRICE

DESIGN PORTFOLIO

Item Name:

NOTES

COMPONENTS	QTY	COST

TOTAL COST
SELLING PRICE

Item Name:

NOTES

COMPONENTS | QTY | COST

TOTAL COST
SELLING PRICE

DESIGN PORTFOLIO

Item Name:

NOTES

COMPONENTS	QTY	COST
	TOTAL COST	
	SELLING PRICE	

Item Name:

NOTES

COMPONENTS | QTY | COST

TOTAL COST
SELLING PRICE

DESIGN PORTFOLIO

Item Name:

NOTES

COMPONENTS	QTY	COST
	TOTAL COST	
	SELLING PRICE	

Item Name:

NOTES

COMPONENTS	QTY	COST

TOTAL COST
SELLING PRICE

DESIGN PORTFOLIO

Item Name:

NOTES

COMPONENTS	QTY	COST

TOTAL COST
SELLING PRICE

Item Name:

NOTES

COMPONENTS	QTY	COST

TOTAL COST
SELLING PRICE

DESIGN PORTFOLIO

Item Name:

NOTES

COMPONENTS	QTY	COST

TOTAL COST	
SELLING PRICE	

Item Name:

NOTES

COMPONENTS | QTY | COST

TOTAL COST
SELLING PRICE

DESIGN PORTFOLIO

Item Name:

NOTES

COMPONENTS	QTY	COST

TOTAL COST

SELLING PRICE

Item Name:

NOTES

COMPONENTS | QTY | COST

TOTAL COST
SELLING PRICE

DESIGN PORTFOLIO

Item Name:

NOTES

COMPONENTS	QTY	COST

TOTAL COST
SELLING PRICE

Item Name:

NOTES

COMPONENTS | QTY | COST

TOTAL COST
SELLING PRICE

DESIGN PORTFOLIO

Item Name:

NOTES

COMPONENTS | QTY | COST

TOTAL COST
SELLING PRICE

Item Name:

NOTES

COMPONENTS	QTY	COST
TOTAL COST		
SELLING PRICE		

DESIGN PORTFOLIO

Item Name:

NOTES

COMPONENTS	QTY	COST

TOTAL COST
SELLING PRICE

Item Name:

NOTES

COMPONENTS | QTY | COST

TOTAL COST
SELLING PRICE

DESIGN PORTFOLIO

Item Name:

NOTES

COMPONENTS	QTY	COST

TOTAL COST
SELLING PRICE

Item Name:

NOTES

COMPONENTS | QTY | COST

TOTAL COST
SELLING PRICE

DESIGN PORTFOLIO

Project:		Source:	
	MATERIALS REQUIRED		COST ESTIMATE
			TIME ESTIMATE
			DEADLINE
STARTED:	FINISHED:		

Project:		Source:	
	MATERIALS REQUIRED		COST ESTIMATE
			TIME ESTIMATE
			DEADLINE
STARTED:	FINISHED:		

Project:		Source:	
	MATERIALS REQUIRED		COST ESTIMATE
			TIME ESTIMATE
			DEADLINE
STARTED:	FINISHED:		

Project: Source:

MATERIALS REQUIRED	COST ESTIMATE
	TIME ESTIMATE
	DEADLINE
STARTED: FINISHED:	

Project: Source:

MATERIALS REQUIRED	COST ESTIMATE
	TIME ESTIMATE
	DEADLINE
STARTED: FINISHED:	

Project: Source:

MATERIALS REQUIRED	COST ESTIMATE
	TIME ESTIMATE
	DEADLINE
STARTED: FINISHED:	

PROJECTS AND IDEAS

Project: **Source:**

MATERIALS REQUIRED	COST ESTIMATE
	TIME ESTIMATE
	DEADLINE

STARTED:	FINISHED:

Project: **Source:**

MATERIALS REQUIRED	COST ESTIMATE
	TIME ESTIMATE
	DEADLINE

STARTED:	FINISHED:

Project: **Source:**

MATERIALS REQUIRED	COST ESTIMATE
	TIME ESTIMATE
	DEADLINE

STARTED:	FINISHED:

Project:		Source:	
MATERIALS REQUIRED			**COST ESTIMATE**
			TIME ESTIMATE
			DEADLINE
STARTED:		FINISHED:	

Project:		Source:	
MATERIALS REQUIRED			**COST ESTIMATE**
			TIME ESTIMATE
			DEADLINE
STARTED:		FINISHED:	

Project:		Source:	
MATERIALS REQUIRED			**COST ESTIMATE**
			TIME ESTIMATE
			DEADLINE
STARTED:		FINISHED:	

PROJECTS AND IDEAS

Project: Source:

MATERIALS REQUIRED	COST ESTIMATE
	TIME ESTIMATE
	DEADLINE

| STARTED: | FINISHED: | |

Project: Source:

MATERIALS REQUIRED	COST ESTIMATE
	TIME ESTIMATE
	DEADLINE

| STARTED: | FINISHED: | |

Project: Source:

MATERIALS REQUIRED	COST ESTIMATE
	TIME ESTIMATE
	DEADLINE

| STARTED: | FINISHED: | |

PROJECTS AND IDEAS

Project: **Source:**

MATERIALS REQUIRED	COST ESTIMATE
	TIME ESTIMATE
	DEADLINE

Started: **Finished:**

Project: **Source:**

MATERIALS REQUIRED	COST ESTIMATE
	TIME ESTIMATE
	DEADLINE

Started: **Finished:**

Project: **Source:**

MATERIALS REQUIRED	COST ESTIMATE
	TIME ESTIMATE
	DEADLINE

Started: **Finished:**

Project:		Source:	
MATERIALS REQUIRED			COST ESTIMATE
			TIME ESTIMATE
			DEADLINE
STARTED:		FINISHED:	

Project:		Source:	
MATERIALS REQUIRED			COST ESTIMATE
			TIME ESTIMATE
			DEADLINE
STARTED:		FINISHED:	

Project:		Source:	
MATERIALS REQUIRED			COST ESTIMATE
			TIME ESTIMATE
			DEADLINE
STARTED:		FINISHED:	

Project: **Source:**

MATERIALS REQUIRED	COST ESTIMATE
	TIME ESTIMATE
	DEADLINE

STARTED: **FINISHED:**

Project: **Source:**

MATERIALS REQUIRED	COST ESTIMATE
	TIME ESTIMATE
	DEADLINE

STARTED: **FINISHED:**

Project: **Source:**

MATERIALS REQUIRED	COST ESTIMATE
	TIME ESTIMATE
	DEADLINE

STARTED: **FINISHED:**

PROJECTS AND IDEAS

Project: **Source:**

MATERIALS REQUIRED	COST ESTIMATE
	TIME ESTIMATE
	DEADLINE
STARTED: **FINISHED:**	

Project: **Source:**

MATERIALS REQUIRED	COST ESTIMATE
	TIME ESTIMATE
	DEADLINE
STARTED: **FINISHED:**	

Project: **Source:**

MATERIALS REQUIRED	COST ESTIMATE
	TIME ESTIMATE
	DEADLINE
STARTED: **FINISHED:**	

PROJECTS AND IDEAS

Project: **Source:**

MATERIALS REQUIRED	COST ESTIMATE
	TIME ESTIMATE
	DEADLINE

STARTED: **FINISHED:**

Project: **Source:**

MATERIALS REQUIRED	COST ESTIMATE
	TIME ESTIMATE
	DEADLINE

STARTED: **FINISHED:**

Project: **Source:**

MATERIALS REQUIRED	COST ESTIMATE
	TIME ESTIMATE
	DEADLINE

STARTED: **FINISHED:**

PROJECTS AND IDEAS

PROJECTS AND IDEAS

PROJECTS AND IDEAS

PROJECTS AND IDEAS

PROJECTS AND IDEAS

PROJECTS AND IDEAS

PROJECTS AND IDEAS

PROJECTS AND IDEAS

PROJECTS AND IDEAS

PROJECTS AND IDEAS

PROJECTS AND IDEAS

PROJECTS AND IDEAS

PROJECTS AND IDEAS

PROJECTS AND IDEAS

PROJECTS AND IDEAS

ITEM	COLOUR	SIZE

WHERE BOUGHT	TOTAL COST	QUANTITY	COST PER ITEM

INVENTORY

ITEM	COLOUR	SIZE

WHERE BOUGHT	TOTAL COST	QUANTITY	COST PER ITEM

INVENTORY

ITEM	COLOUR	SIZE

WHERE BOUGHT	TOTAL COST	QUANTITY	COST PER ITEM

INVENTORY

ITEM	COLOUR	SIZE

WHERE BOUGHT	TOTAL COST	QUANTITY	COST PER ITEM

INVENTORY

ITEM	COLOUR	SIZE

WHERE BOUGHT	TOTAL COST	QUANTITY	COST PER ITEM

INVENTORY

ITEM	COLOUR	SIZE

WHERE BOUGHT	TOTAL COST	QUANTITY	COST PER ITEM

INVENTORY

ITEM	COLOUR	SIZE

WHERE BOUGHT	TOTAL COST	QUANTITY	COST PER ITEM

INVENTORY

BEADS	FINDINGS	THREAD

TOOLS	STORAGE AND PACKAGING	OTHER
○	○	○
○	○	○
○	○	○
○	○	○
○	○	○
○	○	○
○	○	○
○	○	○
○	○	○
○	○	○
○	○	○
○	○	○
○	○	○
○	○	○
○	○	○
○	○	○
○	○	○
○	○	○
○	○	○
○	○	○
○	○	○
○	○	○
○	○	○
○	○	○
○	○	○

NOTES AND LISTS

BEADS	FINDINGS	THREAD

TOOLS	STORAGE AND PACKAGING	OTHER
○	○	○
○	○	○
○	○	○
○	○	○
○	○	○
○	○	○
○	○	○
○	○	○
○	○	○
○	○	○
○	○	○
○	○	○
○	○	○
○	○	○
○	○	○
○	○	○
○	○	○
○	○	○
○	○	○
○	○	○
○	○	○
○	○	○

NOTES AND LISTS

BEADS	FINDINGS	THREAD

TOOLS	STORAGE AND PACKAGING	OTHER
○	○	○
○	○	○
○	○	○
○	○	○
○	○	○
○	○	○
○	○	○
○	○	○
○	○	○
○	○	○
○	○	○
○	○	○
○	○	○
○	○	○
○	○	○
○	○	○
○	○	○
○	○	○
○	○	○
○	○	○
○	○	○

NOTES AND LISTS

NOTES AND LISTS

NOTES AND LISTS

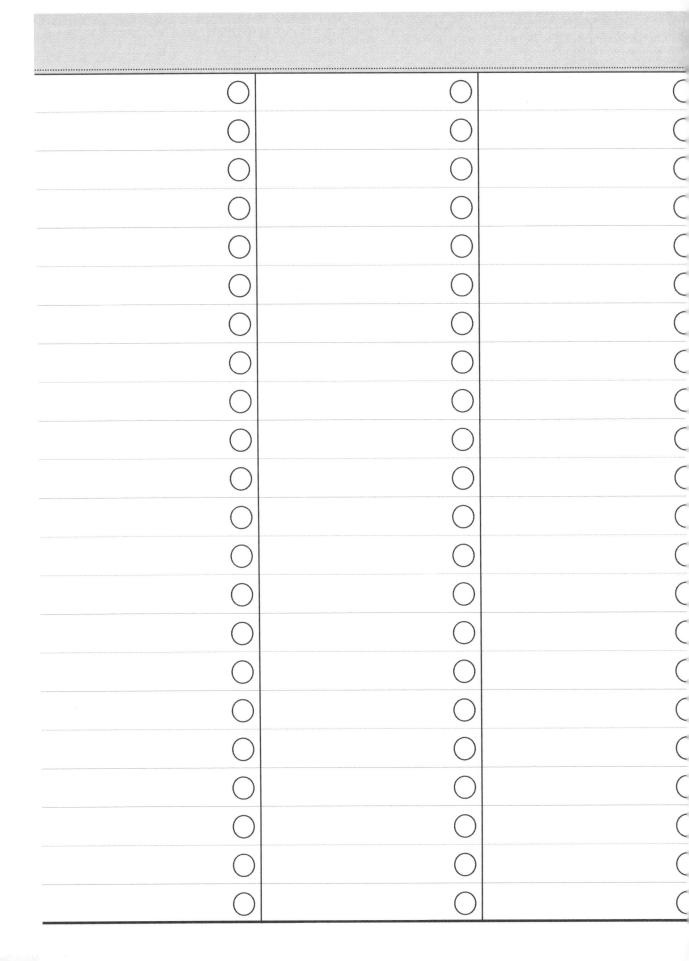

Notes

Notes

Notes

Notes

Notes

Printed in Great Britain
by Amazon

34495622R00075